Sir Isaac Newton

© Copyright 2016 by From Hero To Zero - All rights reserved.

The follow eBook is reproduced below with the goal of providing information that is as accurate and reliable as possible. Regardless, purchasing this eBook can be seen as consent to the fact that both the publisher and the author of this book are in no way experts on the topics discussed within and that any recommendations or suggestions that are made herein are for entertainment purposes only. Professionals should be consulted as needed prior to undertaking any of the action endorsed herein.

This declaration is deemed fair and valid by both the American Bar Association and the Committee of Publishers Association and is legally binding throughout the United States.

Furthermore, the transmission, duplication or reproduction of any of the following work including specific information will be considered an illegal act irrespective of if it is done electronically or in print. This extends to creating a secondary or tertiary copy of the work or a recorded copy and is only allowed with express written consent from the Publisher. All additional right reserved.

The information in the following pages is broadly considered to be a truthful and accurate account of facts and as such any inattention, use or misuse of the information in question by the reader will render any resulting actions solely under their purview. There are no scenarios in which the publisher or the original author of this work can be in any fashion deemed liable for any hardship or damages that may befall them after undertaking information described herein.

Additionally, the information in the following pages is intended only for informational purposes and should thus be thought of as universal. As befitting its nature, it is presented without assurance regarding its prolonged validity or interim quality. Trademarks that are mentioned are done without written consent and can in no way be considered an endorsement from the trademark holder.

Table of Contents

Introduction 1

Isaac Newton: The Early Life 5

Isaac Newton was not a Good Student........................ 7

Isaac Newton's Higher Education Experience..........13

Newton's Scientific Discoveries 19

Newton's Laws.. 23

The Apple Myth 29

Newton Stuck a Needle in his Eye............................. 33

Robert Hooke 37

Gottfried Leibniz 41

Did Isaac Newton Ever Marry? 45

The Gold Standard 47

Isaac Newton, Alchemy, and Magic 51

Newton's Religious Beliefs 55

Newton's Final Years... 59

Newton's Students... 63

Isaac Newton's Legacy... 65

Introduction

Sir Isaac Newton is one of the great characters of scientific history. Not only did he have some of the most important insights, create inventions that are still used all over the world today, and pioneer the use of experiments to develop scientific knowledge, but he is also simply one of the most recognizable figures.

Portraits painted during his life show a handsome man with an intense expression and long flowing hair. Both at the time he lived and in the centuries afterwards, Newton was considered one of the greatest minds in history. Scientists both old and modern use him as one of their great sources of inspiration (Albert Einstein kept a portrait of Newton in his office as motivation when he was working).

Alexander Pope, one of England's most famous poets, who lived at the same time as Newton, elevated him to a mystical Christ-like platform in his famous couplet, written at the time of Newton's death:

**Nature and nature's laws lay hid in night;
God said "Let Newton be" and all was light.**

There can be no doubt that Newton was one of the most important, pivotal figures in science. Yet, in spite of this, most people don't know much about Newton except that he was the

Sir Isaac Newton

scientist who discovered gravity. Who was this great man, really?

The truth is that Isaac Newton was far more complex than the simple genius who illuminated the world with his discoveries that we see. In his childhood, people did not believe that he was likely to amount to much. Not until he started developing and publishing his ground-breaking theories did anyone pay any attention to the young man from Lincolnshire.

But even after he gained his fame, all was not smooth sailing for Newton. He was famously antisocial, and alienated many of the other scientists who were working at the same time as him. He also developed some religious and spiritual beliefs that would be considered odd today and would have been grounds for execution when he was alive. He was just as interested in finding the key to eternal life as he was in figuring out why things fall down instead of up, but the latter has gotten a lot more attention in science classes than the former.

So who was Isaac Newton? Was he a great genius, restrained from even greater success by the conventions of his time and place? Was he a curmudgeon, whose intelligence shielded him from the need to take responsibility for his behaviour? Was he an eccentric would-be magician, whose insights into science were only a by-product of his search for the strange and mystical?

The answer is more complicated than any of these. Newton was a brilliant mind, but he was also a flawed human whose values and interests were, like any of ours, imperfect. By reading this book, you will learn about the facts of Newton's life and the basics of his greatest discoveries. But you will also learn more about Newton, the man. He wasn't just a machine

Introduction

who sat in a room and developed theories. He was a real person who lived and breathed. No matter how important and influential his scientific ideas were (and they were *extremely* important and influential), there was more to Newton than gravity and calculus. Read on to learn more about both the scientist, and the man underneath.

Isaac Newton: The Early Life

The year was 1642 in the tiny town of Woolsthorpe-by-Colsterworth in Lincolnshire, England. A wealthy farmer named Isaac Newton had just died of unknown causes, but it was most probably one of the many diseases that were rampant in England at the time. He had left behind his heavily pregnant wife, Hannah Ayscough. On Christmas, she gave birth prematurely. No one expected the baby to survive. He was so tiny that Hannah claimed he could fit inside a quart mug. She named him Isaac Newton, after his father.

Not much is known about the lives of Isaac Newton Sr. or Hannah Ayscough. Isaac Newton Sr. was called "wild and extravagant," but we don't know what he did to earn that description. His farms were prosperous, and he and his wife resided in the Woolsthorpe Manor. Isaac Newton Sr. died about three months before Hannah gave birth, but fortunately, his wealth was able to continue to support her after his death. Unlike many widows, who did not necessarily have the rights to their husbands' property, Hannah was not forced to rely on charity or the church for support. She and her mother, Margery Ayscough, raised young Isaac in relatively comfortable circumstances.

When the young Isaac was three years old, Hannah remarried, this time to a reverend named Barnabus Smith. She gave Isaac to her mother, who took care of him at Woolsthorpe Manor, while Hannah and Barnabus moved a few miles away to Barnabus's own home. The family remained tightly connected, even though they were not all living in the same household. After Barnabus's death, Hannah returned to live with Margery and Isaac.

Isaac didn't seem to get along very well with either his mother or his stepfather. By leaving Isaac at Woolsthorpe Manor, Hannah made it possible for him to keep his title as lord of the manor, but that didn't change the fact that she was essentially abandoning her son. When he was nineteen, he wrote a list of all his previous sins, which included "threatening my father and mother to burn them and the house over them." Even after Barnabus's death, Isaac seemed to have maintained some distance from his mother. By then, she had three other children from Barnabus who Isaac didn't seem particularly fond of. She also didn't support his education, which drove a wedge between them later in his life.

Isaac Newton was not a Good Student

When he was twelve years old, Isaac became an apprentice to an apothecary (a pharmacist, who studied medicine and chemistry) named William Clarke. Clarke lived about eight miles away from Woolsthorpe, so Isaac stayed in his home and experienced his work up-close and personally. It was during his time working with Clarke that Isaac began to become interested in the natural world. He was a curious child, and Clarke encouraged him to try new things and experiment with new possibilities.

Around the same time, Isaac also enrolled in The King's School in the nearby town of Grantham. The King's School offered the best education available to young men who weren't from the nobility at this time in British history. It was a type of school known as a *grammar school*, which was the equivalent of a modern elementary or junior high school.

Grammar schools were originally founded, hundreds of years before Isaac ever entered one, to teach students Latin. Since about the year 1000 AD (more than 600 years before Newton entered school), everyone educated in Europe had to speak Latin – it was the language of religion, science, and law. Latin was also a *lingua franca*, meaning that people in many different countries, whose native languages were very different, could all understand each other by speaking Latin.

Sir Isaac Newton

Political discussions, news, and any other kind of important information that had to travel across national borders was translated into Latin. That made this language one of the most important things that anyone could learn.

When Isaac was attending The King's School, it might have also taught subjects like Ancient Greek, science, math, and history, which many grammar schools had expanded to include in their curriculums in the hundreds of years since they were first developed. The King's School was prestigious, and known for its excellent teaching. There were opportunities to study great works with great teachers. But no matter what The King's School taught, Isaac didn't find himself very interested in his classes.

His teachers complained that he was "idle" and didn't pay attention to them. In spite of his bright personality, he was not diligent about completing work, and he did not seem to have very much respect for authority. He skipped classes. He didn't take his lessons seriously. The work he did was good, but no one could force him into actually doing it. He also didn't make friends with the other students and was fairly socially isolated, which was a problem that he continued to have throughout his life.

When Isaac was sixteen, his mother Hannah took him out of school. His grades were poor, and while his apprenticeship with William Clarke was promising, being an apothecary was not the most respectable or lucrative career in the 1600s. Instead, she thought that Isaac would do better as a farmer, like his father had been.

Isaac hated farming. He complained that it was boring and monotonous, and he intentionally did even worse at the work that he was given on the farms than he had done in his grammar school. Maybe it was his experience with farming that finally convinced him to apply himself to his education at The King's School. After less than two years on the farm, the headmaster of The King's School, Henry Stokes, wrote to Hannah, asking for Isaac to be sent back, to continue his formal education.

From then on, Isaac became much more successful in his academics. Although he remained slightly rebellious by nature, he was no longer constantly missing from classes, and from the notebooks he kept throughout his life, it appeared to be around this time that he started thinking about subjects on his own time. Maybe he saw that the monotony of schoolwork was nothing compared to the monotony of the job he would have to do if he couldn't be successful in grammar school.

Some modern scholars suspect that, judging by his troublesome behaviour during his childhood and his time at The King's School, Newton was displaying signs of Asperger's Syndrome. Asperger's Syndrome is a form of high-functioning autism that can impair people's sense of social normalcy. It can also contribute to anxiety and stress, since one of the key features of autistic spectrum disorders is that they make it difficult to filter out irrelevant "white noise" from one's environment. All of these features seem somewhat consistent with Newton's behaviour as a child – and as an adult.

Isaac was thirsty for knowledge, but did poorly in the rigid classroom environment of The King's School. He was secretive, and became quickly absorbed in his own work, rather than sharing it with other people. He also displayed paranoid and anxious tendencies, especially later in his life as his mental and physical health deteriorated in his old age.

Sir Isaac Newton

While it's impossible to diagnose someone a few hundred years after their death, the evidence is compelling that Isaac's brain might not have been quite like his peers'. He was extremely prone to questioning conventional knowledge, and was quick to dismiss things that other people thought were great, wise insights, as simplistic nonsense.

Another issue that Newton probably had with school, whether or not he was displaying signs of Asperger's Syndrome, was the way that the schools of his time period approached knowledge. Newton lived in the later part of the Renaissance period, which was known for its developments in art and culture. The Renaissance was a wonderful time to be an artist, but it wasn't always a great time to be a scientist. Rather than being interested in trying new things and looking forward, people of the Renaissance were mostly interested in looking back to the ancient and classical world, and trying to use their knowledge to develop a better society.

The developments that were made in science during the Renaissance weren't because people were discovering new things through experiments, but because they were returning to ancient texts, written by great scientists of Ancient Greece, Rome, Egypt, and Persia. These books were full of information that had been forgotten over the centuries.

The primary way to gather information in the Renaissance was to read the works of these ancient scientists and use the principles they discovered to try to come to new conclusions about the universe. Experiments weren't particularly popular, and it was practically taboo to try to disagree with any of these thinkers, even if they said things that made no sense based on what people experienced about the world. It was because of this unwillingness to question the wisdom of the ancients that science actually stagnated during the Renaissance period.

Isaac Newton was not a Good Student

Newton lived almost at the very end of the Renaissance period, and for the last hundred years, more scientists were trying to develop more new ideas and question some of the conventional wisdom of the time. However, these thinkers were still in the minority, and they struggled to make their conclusions heard – and their methods of experimentation were completely out of fashion.

The process of looking back on old thinkers rather than trying to come up with new or better information through experiments clearly didn't sit well with Newton. He had already learned from William Clarke's work as an apothecary that it was important to experiment and try new things in order to achieve greater success or improve upon old knowledge. Newton's resistance to copying the wisdom of the ancients would certainly have served him poorly in school where new ideas were not rewarded, but knowledge of classic texts was.

His teachers mainly seemed to think that Isaac was simply stubborn and unwilling to learn. But some specific stories about his youth indicate that it was actually his unusually curious and critical nature, and his natural intelligence, that made him so unwilling to sit down and learn what his teachers assigned to him.

According to one story, Isaac picked up a copy of the book *Elements* by the famous Ancient Greek mathematician Euclid. Euclid is known today as "the father of geometry" because of how huge his contributions to the field were. In the Renaissance, Euclid was one of the most significant of the many great ancient thinkers that were held in such high regard. He was seen practically as a god – his ideas were worshipped above all others in the field of mathematical studies.

Sir Isaac Newton

Apparently, Newton spent only a short while reading the book before he decided that Euclid wasn't telling him anything that he didn't already know, or couldn't have easily figured out with a bit of logical thought. He dismissed *Elements*, which was the foundation of his curriculum at school, as "a trifling book" and moved on to contemporary thinkers instead, deciding that the ancients were hardly worth his time.

His dismissal came back to bite him later though – when he was graduating from university, he had to take an exam on Euclid, which he didn't do well on. Over time, Newton developed a degree of greater respect for the ancient thinkers, but unlike so many of the scientists of the Renaissance, he refused to ever take their word for absolute truth. Instead, he used their ideas as a basis to develop his own theories, and put them to the test as rigorously as possible.

When he was a child, no one would have guessed that Isaac was going to grow up to be one of the greatest geniuses of history. The cards were stacked against him from the beginning. In the 1600s, it was very rare for a child who was born prematurely to make a recovery. His bad relationship with his mother and stepfather, and his difficulties in making friends and building relationships with people also would have caused serious damage to a less forceful personality. However, while his social relationships were few and far between, and his relationships to his teachers were not great, no one could deny that the scientific work that Isaac Newton was doing, and the conclusions he was coming to, were going to turn out to be important.

Isaac Newton's Higher Education Experience

Although Isaac's early educational career got off to a slow start when he was attending grammar school, his apprenticeship to William Clarke did spark an interest in science. Ironically, in the 1600s, apothecaries were doing much more scientific research (as we would understand the idea of "scientific research" today) than schools or universities were doing. While schools took almost all their information from "the classical authorities" like the works of Euclid, apothecaries actually had a reason to care about finding out new information – so that they could save more lives with their medicine.

While it is, of course, very important to study what other people have written in the past, especially in a field like science that requires a strong foundation of knowledge in order to make new discoveries, schools in the 1600s weren't very interested in testing the information that they read. They also weren't very interested in learning new things, especially things that weren't suggested by the ancient texts. Today, some teachers are concerned that school curriculums only teach students how to repeat information rather than think for themselves – in the Renaissance, that was the entire model!

This turned out to be an enormous problem in the Renaissance, because some of the writers that Renaissance thinkers were taking as perfectly accurate authorities turned out to have rather poor grasps on science. While some ideas had merit, some were inaccurate, and the Renaissance thinkers had no good mechanisms for separating the useful ones from the ones that were holding back the development of society.

For example, like most people in Ancient Greece, Aristotle (the absolute highest of all the classical authorities of the Renaissance) was convinced that the Sun revolved around the Earth. According to his model, the Earth was a stationary object, and the planets orbited in concentric circles around it, with the stars (essentially unmoving) far beyond that. Although a cursory study of astronomy at least would call this into question, this theory was still held up as absolute truth for centuries. Aristotle was so emphatic on this point that it took a long time and many ruined reputations before anyone could convince the general scientific community to think of the cosmos in any way other than the one he described.

While cosmic misconceptions like this can at least be justified because correct answers would be very hard to find and prove, some of Aristotle's theories were not only flat-out incorrect, but also easily corrected with simple experiments. For example, Aristotle claimed that heavier objects fell faster than lighter ones, even though a very straightforward experiment could prove otherwise. "Experiments" weren't really Aristotle's field of interest.

The famous scientist Galileo Galilei disproved Aristotle's theory about mass about a hundred years before Newton lived with one of the simplest experiments in history (he simply dropped two balls, one heavier than the other, from the Leaning Tower of Pisa – and, indeed, they hit the ground at the same time). It was a huge step towards disassembling the educational system that took everything an ancient authority said at face value. However, even though Galileo's experiment had clearly proven that Aristotle wasn't always correct about everything and that it could be very easy to test his theories, the classical authorities were still upheld as the most important sources of knowledge in the world.

It was easy for schools to keep up this method of thinking – after all, they didn't really have to apply any of the information they claimed was accurate. On the other hand, apothecaries had a very good reason to want to experiment and try new things – if your medicine doesn't work, then no one will want to buy it! William Clarke, like most Renaissance apothecaries, was not only willing, but *eager,* to try new things. Long before Newton went to school, Clarke was teaching him how important this was, and instilling what we would now call "scientific curiosity" in him.

Clarke encouraged Isaac to study and experiment with chemistry, and to think about the role of science and math in the world. He encouraged him to question what he was told and try to test it out for himself. Thanks to Clarke's encouragement, Newton threw himself enthusiastically into independent study and learned a great deal about chemistry and math, both from Clarke's work and from reading the works of contemporary thinkers who were a little less attached to Aristotle than Newton's teachers were.

When Isaac was 19 years old, he went to Cambridge University to take on a work-study position – the only way that promising students from families that weren't noble could afford to go to the prestigious university. His mother still wished that he had become a farmer, and his relationship with her was rather poor, so he was not receiving the financial aid that the son of a prosperous farmer might have expected.

Sir Isaac Newton

Newton became a *sizar*, which was (and still remains, even in the twenty-first century) Cambridge's term for a student who receives financial aid (or room and board) in exchange for doing some kind of work for the university. Most sizars were the children of poor parents, and although Newton's background was comparatively prosperous, he joined them in doing menial labour, cooking, and cleaning in the university kitchens in exchange for his education.

Technically, Newton was interested in studying law at Cambridge, but at that time, a university education meant studying a huge variety of topics, from law and theology, to math and medicine. He developed a greater interest in the sciences during this time, and was enthusiastic about studying them and learning more so that he could make contributions to the field. During his studies, he developed a lot of the background knowledge that would later make his great discoveries possible.

Most of what Cambridge taught at that time was, however, still based on the work of Aristotle. We've already talked a bit about Aristotle and his questionable scientific discoveries, and Newton had already revealed that he was skeptical of even the most readily accepted authorities. Newton, like any modern thinker, was not very impressed by Aristotle's science. He was, however, impressed at Galileo, who had given up his reputation in order to put Aristotle's ideas to the test.

Rather than taking Aristotle's ideas at face value like his peers did, Newton used ideas from more recent philosophers, like Galileo, René Descartes (the writer who said "I think, therefore I am"), and Copernicus (the originator of the idea that the sun was at the centre of the solar system). However, even with his favourite thinkers, Newton never took anyone else's ideas as absolute truth. He was always interested in questioning and testing the information for himself. He even once said, famously, "Plato is my friend. Aristotle is my friend. But my greatest friend is truth."

In 1665, just after Isaac graduated, Cambridge had to shut down in reaction to the Great Plague of London. The Great Plague was a resurgence of the Black Death (which had killed hundreds of thousands in the Middle Ages). This cut Isaac off from his university's resources, so instead, he continued his studies at home. Freed from the control of any professors, he was able to explore his ideas with even more curiosity, and take more intellectual risks than he had been able to at school. He read voraciously, and developed new theories about math and science based on what he learned.

Isaac kept notebooks that he called "commonplace books" during this time, which he filled up with the information he was learning and the ideas he was having. His commonplace books included his thoughts, notes, and observations, as well as passages from books he was reading and comments on them. Isaac called them his "waste books," but he had no way of knowing how useful they'd be in a few hundred years. Now, historians know exactly what he was interested in during this time in his life.

In entries from 1664, he was writing about calculus, music, his observations of the moon, and his ideas about other people's mathematical theories. Some of his notes went on to be revised and published in his many books, especially his most famous *Philosophiae Naturalis Principia Mathematica*, or *The Mathematical Principles of Natural Philosophy*. In these books, he used his observational notes and ideas about people's theories as the bases for new theories about both mathematics and the natural world.

Sir Isaac Newton

In his twenties, Newton carried out a wide range of experiments about which not very much is known. There are records of him buying materials, like prisms and chemicals, but we don't know exactly what he was studying or what sort of conclusions he came to at this time. It is possible that this was when he first began experimenting with alchemy and magic, which was highly taboo during Newton's lifetime, and therefore he would have very good reason to try to conceal it. Magic became one of Newton's major interests later in his life, and his magical studies will be discussed in the chapter "Isaac Newton, Alchemy, and Magic."

During this time of independent study, Newton also studied and wrote about pure math. He developed new theories and equations to try to explain some more complex ideas that mathematics were having difficulty expressing at the time. In 1669, he gave a paper he had written on the study of equations to a professor of mathematics, who passed it on to a famous mathematician named John Collins. Newton's name was not on the paper, but the professor assured Collins that the paper was written by a "powerful genius." Only after Collins had said how impressed he was with the paper did the professor reveal who had written it, impressing Collins with Newton's brilliance and innovation. It was thanks to this professor's help that Newton was able to take on the job as the Lucasian Professor of Mathematics, a prestigious position at the university that allowed him to have some job security while he pursued his studies further.

Newton's Scientific Discoveries

After Newton had some security in his position as a Professor of Mathematics, he was able to devote much more serious study to his experiments and inventions.

Over the course of his scientific career, Newton made many discoveries in the fields of science, math, and more that are still crucial to modern scientists, mathematicians, and everyday people. Some of his discoveries are well known – and some are even named after him – but he also invented some lesser-known things that you may not have even known were his ideas.

One of Newton's biggest innovations was in the field of calculus. Before Newton was alive, "calculus" just meant "mathematics" – anything involving numbers, whether that was basic arithmetic or complex geometry. However, as understandings of the world and universe became more complex, people began to find that the mathematical principles they were using at the time were not up to the challenges of explaining the world. Around the time that Newton was alive, mathematicians in Europe were becoming more and more interested in math as a type of philosophy. They were looking at math through the eyes of modern (at the time) thinkers, and were trying to use it to answer more complicated problems about the world.

Sir Isaac Newton

While Newton was studying at Cambridge and thinking very carefully about subjects like physics, he realized that he needed a separate field to describe some of the things that he was discovering. He noticed that the motion could be described with scientific and mathematical formulas. The formulas that he developed to describe motion became the basis for his theories of calculus.

Although Newton's ideas about calculus proved to be extremely useful, there was a problem in getting the information out to the world. Because it was very difficult for all of these new mathematical thinkers to communicate with each other, the information they were collecting was not very well organized. They all used different theories and techniques as the bases for their mathematical writing, and there also wasn't any consistency in how they expressed their discoveries. Therefore, the most important thing that someone could do in the mathematical community was publish their theories in a clear, readable way, that other mathematicians and thinkers would see and read from, and which would then influence their own writings.

Isaac Newton was also very interested in the eyes, and especially in lenses. When he was just 25 years old, he invented a type of telescope known as a reflecting telescope, which used a very simple design with mirrors and lenses to magnify objects at great distances.

Newton's telescopes were much clearer, more portable, and more accurate than the telescopes that had been in use before. The old style of telescopes were called "refracting telescopes" and they were extremely large and unwieldy pieces of machinery that gave only blurry visions of far-away objects.

By creating a telescope that was small, portable, unusually clear, and relatively easy to manufacture, Newton helped popularize astronomy as a subject of general interest. He encouraged more people to look at the sky and pay attention to the way that the stars seemed to move.

According to the model of the universe proposed by Aristotle, which was still the generally understood model of the universe in Newton's lifetime, the Earth is essentially a stationary ball around which all the other heavenly bodies rotate. This idea had been called into question by natural philosophers like Copernicus and Galileo over the last few centuries before Newton, but it was still popularly held. However, as astronomical equipment like the reflecting telescope became more available, more people became interested in the workings of the heavens. They started paying more attention and seeing patterns and inconsistencies in Aristotle's theory more clearly. Through this, Newton's invention of the telescope contributed to popularizing the *heliocentric* model of the universe – the idea that the Earth revolves around the Sun, rather than the other way around.

Newton wrote an entire book about lenses and light, including some of the scientific discoveries involved in his invention of the reflecting telescope. The book was called *Opticks: or, a treatise on the reflexions, refractions, inflexions and colours of light*. It contains descriptions of many of Newton's experiments related to light, colour, and vision. Its main subject is *diffraction*, which is the way that light deals with obstacles, by either bending around or through them. Newton's word for this set of reactions between light and the physical world was *inflexion*. The theories that he put forward in *Opticks* were almost entirely new, and have been indispensable for the study of light in science. When it came out, *Opticks* was considered just as great a work as Newton's previous book about science, the *Philosophiae Naturalis Principia Mathematica*.

Unfortunately for Newton, when *Opticks* was published in 1704, it sparked the onset of a major legal battle that Newton ended up fighting with his rival scientist, Gottfried Leibniz. This battle distracted the public somewhat from the content of the book, which has never risen quite to the level of the *Principia* in terms of fame.

Opticks also included a set of short essays by Newton called the Queries, which related (either closely or tangentially) to the main subject of the book. They were more theoretical and less clearly supported by empirical evidence than the work that Newton generally published, but they still presented some fascinating theories about things like the cause of gravity, and even the nature of human ethics. The Queries were where Newton most became a philosopher, and least a "scientist" as we would think of it today. However, remember that the term for a scientist in the Renaissance was a "natural philosopher!" While this was an unusual move for Newton, many of his contemporaries did similar work, and after he did it, it became quite fashionable to add philosophical musings into scientific works.

Newton's Laws

We have covered several of Newton's most famous inventions and most significant works – but his telescopes and calculus pale in comparison to the importance of his laws about the way in which the natural world operates. If you only know about a couple of Newton's discoveries, though, you probably know about his discovery of the laws of motion and the laws of gravity.

Newton's three laws of motion are probably something that you learned in a science class, not a history class. These laws are:

> **Every object persists in its state of rest or uniform motion in a straight line unless it is compelled to change that state by forces impressed on it.**
>
> **Force is equal to the change in momentum per change in time. For a constant mass, force equals mass x acceleration.**
>
> **For every action, there is an equal and opposite reaction.**

These laws explain the interaction of force and matter. In other words, they describe what happens when you do things to objects. This may seem simple, and it is. It made the ideas

Sir Isaac Newton

of movement much less mysterious than they had been seen as previously.

It was their simplicity that made Newton's laws become so popular, widely known, and influential. Even people with very little background in science can grasp the concepts he explains in his laws. In order, these laws tell us...

> 1) **That nothing will change from its course unless some outside force changes it. (That outside force could be gravity or friction).**
>
> 2) **That force is a combination of weight and speed (so being hit by a feather at high speed and being hit by a truck at slow speed are both better than being hit by a truck at high speed). And,**
>
> 3) **That every movement requires some sort of opposite movement as well.**

Newton was developing his theories about motion in his commonplace books starting when he was only 24 years old. In 1687, when he was in his 40s, he published *Philosophiae Naturalis Principia Mathematica*, or *The Mathematical Principles of Natural Philosophy*, in which he wrote the three laws of motion as we know them today. It also explains a lot of his other theories, based on his experiments and research into other thinkers and mathematicians. The *Philosophiae Naturalis Principia Mathematica* is considered one of the most important books in the entire history of math and science. It's so famous that it has its own nickname – it's almost always just referred to as the *Principia*.

As well as the laws of motion, the *Principia* became famous for one quote from Newton in the conclusion: *Hypotheses non fingo*. This is Latin for "I pretend no hypothesis" – in other words, in this statement, Newton refuses to offer an explanation for why the things are the way they are. He had been prompted, multiple times, to put forward an explanation for why force and matter worked in the ways that he described, but over and over, he said that he could not, and didn't even want to. All that he was really willing to say was "this is how things are." He didn't think that making "educated guesses" was a good idea for someone who had spent their whole life focussing on experiments. He also didn't feel comfortable putting forward a theory about the *whys* when he felt like he didn't have anywhere near enough information about the intricate workings of the world to even *begin* to understand it. Instead, he wanted to leave the question "but *why* are things the way they are?" to future scientists and thinkers.

Newton's laws of motion were extremely famous and absolutely crucial for the development of modern science. But no less important, and possibly even more famous (for its origins more than its content) was Newton's law of universal gravitation.

The law of universal gravitation states that all matter in the universe attracts all other matter in the universe, and the strength of the attraction depends both on their mass and their distance apart.

The most obvious experience of gravity that most people have is the gravitational pull of the Earth, which is very strong. According to Newton's law, the mass of the Earth is enormous and we are really quite close to it, so the gravitational pull that the Earth exerts on us is very strong – strong enough that we physically cannot help but be pulled as far as possible towards the centre (before we are stopped by another piece of matter, like the Earth's crust).

But Newton took it a step farther: smaller, or further-away objects also have gravitational pull, just weaker. The moon is smaller than the Earth, and quite a bit further away, but its gravitational pull is still strong enough to drag on the water of the ocean and create the tides. Extrapolating from big examples like this, Newton figured out that *everything* in the universe has a gravitational pull, even if it seems infinitesimally small.

In the 20th century, Albert Einstein's theories expanded on Newton, taking other factors into account besides just mass and distance. However, Newton's theories remain the most useful for most people in the everyday world trying to figure out how gravity works.

By creating these laws, Newton was able to quantify some of the most complicated features of the natural world. These are the discoveries that, more than anything else, have contributed to Newton being seen as an almost divine figure of genius: no mortal man, many people believe, could understand the world with such perfect clarity as to distill it into simple, graceful rules the way Newton did.

However, if you're not a scientist or a philosopher, you might still find something intriguing about Newton's laws – specifically, Newton's law of gravity. The really exciting thing about Newton's law of gravity, as far as most people in popular culture are concerned, isn't the actual law he discovered, but how he discovered it. The vast majority of people are only slightly interested in the principle that two tiny, little particles could still have gravitational pull towards each other. More people are interested in the notion that the world can be quantified the way that Newton did. But Newton's theory of gravity had another point in its favour besides its scientific and philosophical significance – it came tied up in a highly recognizable and almost mythical story about an apple falling from a tree.

The Apple Myth

It's almost impossible to grow up in the Western world without seeing some representation of Isaac Newton dozing under an apple tree, and an apple falling on his head. You probably saw it long before you had any idea about the theory of gravity. Possibly the only story from scientific history that can rival the apple myth for pop-culture recognisability is Benjamin Franklin flying a kite in a thunderstorm to discover electricity.

The myth of Isaac Newton and the apple goes something like this:

Newton was dozing in his garden, thinking about his experiments. He had hit some kind of roadblock in his study and was struggling to figure out some of the concepts he'd been working on. He was lying underneath an apple tree, thinking about the problems he was facing, and had almost fallen asleep when an apple fell out of the tree and hit him on the head. In that moment of surprise, Newton had a flash of inspiration that caused him to think up the law of universal gravitation.

This story is very appealing on a pure narrative level, even before you understand the significance of gravity. It has everything: dramatic tension, humour, and a graceful self-contained-ness. We love to think that it's possible for something simple to bring on a sudden flash of genius. We also like the idea that a great idea could be "knocked into" someone's head. Even Newton himself understood this, and he promoted the story of being inspired by an apple throughout his later life.

The first written account of Newton being inspired by an apple falling from a tree came from the book *Memoirs of Sir Isaac Newton's Life*, which was written by Newton's friend William Stukeley. The account was based on what Newton told Stukeley when he was visiting him in 1726, about forty years after it is claimed the apple event actually happened.

This is how Stukeley described Newton's explanation of the apple story:

> After dinner, the weather being warm, we went into the garden and drank tea under the shade of some apple tree; only he and myself... amid other discourse, he told me, he was just in the same situation as when formerly the notion of gravitation came into his mind. Why should that apple always descend perpendicularly to the round, thought he to himself... why should it not go sideways, or upwards? But constantly to the Earth's centre? Assuredly the reason is, that the Earth draws it. There must be a drawing power in matter.

According to Newton, this happened in the 1680s. He related the story to Stukeley in 1726, and the book was not published until 1752, three quarters of a century after the event allegedly happened. This was the first clue that most people had that there might be some element of unreliability to the story, but that potential unreliability did nothing to dampen people's enthusiasm for the tale.

The Apple Myth

Newton's story about the apple might have been true, although there were no notes to this effect in his commonplace books from the time. Of course, it's completely possible that he simply never bothered to make note of this particular experience, focussing instead on what he figured out based on it. After Stukeley published his account, several other people related versions of the event that Newton had recounted to them, and it became true that the story had changed over time. Keith Moore, the Royal Society's head of library and archives, who was responsible for restoring Stukeley's manuscript, said that, "Newton cleverly honed this anecdote over time... the story was certainly true, but let's say it got better with the telling."

The idea that an apple falling from a tree could inspire such great insight is more likely to have been a teaching device than a real event. By saying that he was inspired to think about gravity by something so simple, Newton encouraged Stukeley to think about his own world in the same way. Allow the imagination to run wild, Newton seemed to be saying. Let your mind wander and stumble upon bigger questions.

The idea of an apple inspiring great knowledge has a Biblical quality too. After all, in the Book of Genesis in the Bible, humanity "fell" out of God's graces when humans ate the fruit of the Tree of Knowledge, which has commonly been represented as an apple. It may be that Newton – who was a Biblical scholar in his spare time, and very interested in the symbolism of religious texts – was intentionally drawing on religious symbolism to underline his story and draw more attention to it. Perhaps the reference to the Bible is why it "stuck" in the public consciousness more than a story of a falling rock might have – even if this was happening on a purely subconscious level for most people who heard it.

Sir Isaac Newton

The detail about the apple hitting Newton on the head seems to have been an even more recent addition. Stukeley's account says nothing of the sort. Maybe people added that to give the story an element of humour (one of the best ways to make something memorable), or to introduce the idea of Newton being close to sleep and awoken by the apple.

Some more recent writers have theorized that this story was created by Newton in order to disguise his real techniques, which might have been considered dangerous or even satanic by the church at the time (remember, Newton was living just at the tail end of the great series of witch-burnings that swept across Europe in the Renaissance). Michael White claimed in his book, *Newton: The Last Sorcerer,* that the apple myth was a "politically correct" story created to disguise the possibility that Newton developed his theory of gravity while working on an alchemical project, rather than a math problem. However, it's impossible to know whether Newton was really inspired, ultimately, by an apple or by alchemy.

We will probably never know exactly how much of the apple myth really happened, and how much was made up, either by Newton himself or by future biographers or storytellers. What is definitely true is that the image of Newton being hit on the head with an apple is still one of the most famous images in the history of science.

Newton Stuck a Needle in his Eye

One of Isaac Newton's greatest physical inventions was the reflecting telescope. Newton actually first developed this type of telescope to try to prove his theory that white light was made up of many other colours of light. He turned out to be right – but the telescope wasn't quite enough to prove it. In order to try to gather more concrete evidence for this, Newton devised one of his most famous and dangerous experiments.

Newton thought that the lens of the human eyeball created colour out of white light, because lenses were known to refract blue and red light differently. He thought that if he could distort the eyeball slightly, his perceptions of colours might change because the shape of the lens would change and therefore might work differently with the light.

It wasn't a bad theory – but the way that he decided to go about testing it was a bit gory. In 1665, he took a blunt needle, stuck it in between his eyeball and orbital bone (the piece of skull underneath the eye), and used it like a lever to put pressure on the back of his eyeball.

He wrote careful notes about the experience, which have been preserved in his notebooks. He wrote:

> I took a bodkin (needle) and put it betwixt my eye and bone as neare to backside of my eye as I could: and

> pressing my eye [with the] end of it... there appeared several white dark and coloured circles... Which circles were plainest when I continued to rub my eye [with the] point of bodkin, but if I held my eye and bodkin still, though I continued to press my eye [with] it, yet [the] circles would grow faint and often disappear until I removed [them] by moving my eye or [the] bodkin.

Unfortunately, he wasn't able to determine whether colour was created in the eye, but he did discover that, by distorting the back of his eye with the needle, he could make dark patches appear and disappear on his field of vision. The patches were strongest when the back of the eye was being actively rubbed with the point of the needle.

Newton's discovery about the eyeball was certainly interesting, but it can't compare to some of his other scientific discoveries or innovations. The experiment has overshadowed the result. What is far more remarkable than anything he actually discovered about the eye is that, while writing about it, Newton's notes are extremely clear, logical, and have a detached tone. They don't display any of the pain or distress that one might expect from someone taking notes while a needle was pressing the back of their eyeball – in fact, he wrote very clinically (and at length) about the experiment, never once describing any pain or discomfort he might have experienced during it. Even though anaesthetics hadn't been invented yet, it is possible that he found a way to insert the bodkin that didn't disturb any nerves in the area. Alternatively, maybe Newton was just unusually tolerant to pain, or exceptionally good at writing with clarity and control in spite of it.

However, remember, in the 1600s, there was no such thing as antiseptic. For all of Newton's scientific knowledge, he had no idea about all the bacteria that he was smearing into the sensitive tissue of his eye. He probably wouldn't even have thought to wash the needle with soap and water before putting it in his eye (not that the bacteria-filled water or lye soap available at the time would have helped him much). At most, he might have wiped it off with a cloth.

Unsurprisingly, Newton developed an infection in his eye, which further developed into a nasty case of gangrene. It's incredible that it didn't kill him, since gangrene was one of the most dangerous diseases that someone could develop in a time before antiseptics or antibiotics.

Even though Newton was able to handle the experiment at the time, this is certainly *not* an experiment that should be repeated, especially given how little information on the subject of how the eye perceives colour he actually gathered from the experiment.

Robert Hooke

While Isaac Newton was undoubtedly brilliant, he was also not the most personable fellow. He became well-known for getting into fights with other scientists and thinkers about who had an idea first (or who articulated it better). One of the most famous and nastiest of these fights was with a scientist named Robert Hooke.

Robert Hooke was a successful scientist. He had started out as a poor student of natural philosophy, which was the name for what we would now call science. His prospects for success didn't look good. But in 1666, things changed. He was working a job as a surveyor in the city of London when the Great Fire of 1666 hit and destroyed much of the city. Hooke was instrumental in rebuilding London after the fire, and was responsible for many of the great structures that characterized the city over the next two centuries. He was also commended for his honest dealings, and hired by dozens of people as a makeshift lawyer in post-fire property disputes. After showing himself to be a great lawyer, and an even better architect, Hooke was finally able to make a name for himself in science, his true passion.

Hooke got himself in trouble, however, when he trod on Newton's toes. He was doing work on the same type of subjects that Newton was, like gravity, the planets and solar system, and light and lenses. He even came up with the same idea as Newton for calculating gravitational pull – possibly before

Sir Isaac Newton

Newton did. (And almost definitely without an apple falling on his head).

When Newton published the *Principia*, which outlined his theories about gravity, Hooke claimed that he had thought of them first and given Newton the idea. This led to a bitter, decades-long rivalry, with both of them thoroughly attacking the character and the reputation of the other. It got so bad that Isaac Newton allegedly had all portraits of Hooke destroyed when he took over the *Royal Society of London for Improving Natural Knowledge*, of which they were both members. It isn't known whether Newton actually did destroy all the portraits on purpose, but it is a well-documented fact that portraits existed of Hooke when Newton came into office that weren't there when he left.

Hooke was not known to be a very friendly man. He never married, and although he didn't live a reclusive life, many people who knew him complained of his vengeful, jealous, selfish personality. He used codes and ciphers to disguise his writing and experiments out of fear that other people would try to take credit for his work, as he claimed Newton did. When he believed someone had stolen one of his ideas (which was often, because this was a time when many thinkers were coming to the same conclusions at the same time), he was known to fly into violent rages or deep periods of sulking.

While he considered Newton his greatest rival (and it is probable that Newton felt the same way about him, although Hooke might have started it), the two of them actually focussed on very different parts of natural philosophy.

Newton was most interested in coming up with mathematical theories that explained the great questions of the world. His graceful formulae, like "force equals mass times acceleration," are world-famous. He was best known for reducing infinitely complex-seeming ideas into clear, simple, and elegant ideas. While he was interested in conducting experiments, his main field of interest was the theoretical, not the practical.

On the other hand, Robert Hooke was fascinated with what one could describe as the "real world." He mainly studied creatures and plants, not forces, and was especially interested in the tiny, often messy, details of life on Earth. His most famous book was a work called *Micrographia: or Some Physiological Descriptions of Minute Bodies Made by Magnifying Glasses, with Observations and Inquiries Thereupon*. As you might be able to figure out from the title, the entire purpose of this book was to diagram and describe insects and plants through microscopes. Microscopes were a new and exciting invention, but they were really only interesting to people who wanted to study the tiny details of the natural world, not to people who wanted to answer big questions, like "why do we fall down instead of up?"

Some highlights from *Micrographia* include the description of a fly's eye, the first-ever use of the word "cell" to describe the tiny pockets that make up plant structures, and the huge fold-out drawings of insects. The drawings from *Micrographia* are still considered some of the greatest and most detailed pre-photographic evidence of tiny creatures, and Hooke's drawings are still used in science textbooks as visual aids to this day.

Robert Hooke was fascinated by the intricate structures he discovered under the microscope. It was a revelation, to both him and to the people around him, that creatures barely visible to the human eye were anything more than tiny balls of flying matter. For the first time in human history, people were able to truly see how complicated the tiny insects and plants they'd been taking for granted really were. In fact, they were so complex and intricate, and bore so many resemblances to other, larger creatures, that Hooke began to think about how they got that way. He wondered how something could be so tiny, and yet have so many moving parts that reminded him of the structures of larger insects and invertebrates, and even of some large animals. Because of his research, Hooke became one of the world's first proponents of the theory of evolution, long before Charles Darwin wrote about it.

Maybe he and Newton could have peacefully coexisted, with Newton focussing on physics and mathematics and Hooke focussing on living creatures and evolution. There were other scholars doing far more consistently similar work that they might have had more reason to be jealous and suspicious of. But it was not to be.

Perhaps it was more about their personalities than their scientific research. Both Hooke and Newton were accused of being cantankerous, jealous, possessive, and generally rude. They were not always enemies – in fact, they started out on relatively good terms (it was in a letter to Hooke that Newton wrote his famous – and famously modest – quote, "if I have seen further, it is by standing on the shoulders of giants"). But they brought out the worst in each other, especially in their declining years, when both of them were suffering from physical and mental degeneration. The arguments and slanders that passed between them were intense and violent, and Newton clearly came out on top as the more "respectable" scientist. It wasn't until the twentieth century that anyone even made an effort to salvage Hooke's reputation, and he still remains far lesser-known than his contemporaries.

Gottfried Leibniz

Robert Hooke wasn't the only well-known scientist that Newton had a feud with. For decades, Newton was also embroiled in a rivalry with another mathematician – a German named Gottfried Leibniz.

Leibniz could not have been a more different man from Newton. Newton was an embittered, tortured genius, who suffered from more than one extended mental breakdown. Leibniz has not been as well-remembered for his scientific discoveries as Newton. On the other hand, he was very well-known for his good manners, his wide circle of friends and admirers, and his philosophical optimism.

The late Renaissance, when both Newton and Leibniz were doing their work, was a time of great philosophical unrest. There had been an enormous rift festering for years between people who adhered to Catholicism as a religion, and people who were following the new type of Christianity; Protestantism. Because of the serious unrest that was happening between these two groups, a lot of philosophers were proposing increasingly cynical views of the world. People wondered whether there was any truth at all to religion, or if perhaps the world, which was so full of sadness and distress, might be ruled by the Devil rather than a benevolent God. This stress was why there was so much religious persecution in the Renaissance, including thousands of witch burnings.

Leibniz couldn't propose a perfect solution to all the issues of religious tension. However, he did argue strongly in his work that the world that we live in was, *"die beste aller möglichen Welten,"* or "the best of all possible worlds." He wrote an entire book on the subject, called *Essays on the Goodness of God, the Freedom of Man, and the Origin of Evil*.

Leibniz's argument, which uses the Bible to back up all his statements, essentially states:

> God can only choose one universe that actually exists.
> God makes choices based on reason, and is good.
> Therefore, there is no explanation except that the universe that exists is the best one possible.

Why, however, one might wonder, couldn't God have created a world with less evil in it? Leibniz argued that the universe as we experience it actually has the perfect balance of good and evil – just enough evil to create the greatest amount of goodness, and contrast the goodness so that we can understand it.

Clearly, Leibniz was a chronic optimist, which made him a rather different type of philosopher from Newton, who (while certainly not pessimistic) wasn't very interested in answering the questions of God – much less coming up with such unremittingly positive explanations for why things are the way they are.

While Leibniz and Newton clashed over their philosophical principles, that wasn't the real reason for their feud. When Leibniz was visiting London on his travels, he spent some time with Newton, and, Newton claimed, got a sneak peek at Newton's mathematical work. A few years later, both Newton and Leibniz published work on the same subject: what we now call calculus.

The core of the issue was simply that Leibniz happened to be doing similar things with mathematical calculations to what Newton was working on. They weren't even identical methods – Ivor Grattan-Guinness even stated in *The Norton History of the Mathematical Sciences* that their methods "are profoundly different, so making the priority row a nonsense." However, although there was plenty of room in the mathematics community for both of them, a serious controversy appeared, mostly in the latter parts of their lives, about which one of them could claim to have actually "invented" calculus.

In 1699, a Swiss mathematician accused Leibniz of stealing the ideas for calculus from Newton, to very little impact. However, much more drama ensued in 1704, when an anonymous review of Newton's work suggested that *Newton* might have been the plagiarist. This set off a spark between the two thinkers that led to a nine-year debate and lawsuit. Despite the fact that the review had virtually no credibility, both sides viciously attacked each other, both claiming to have had the idea first, and to have had it stolen. Newton even had his friends release an entire book summarizing his case against Leibniz.

In general, history has favoured Newton over Leibniz (no one ever wrote a poem saying "God said 'let Leibniz be' and all was light"). However, it is not only possible, but *probable,* that they managed to have the ideas independently. Leibniz's supporters took some comfort in the fact that his notation for calculus was widely accepted to be clearer and more useful than Newton's notation, and so has become the standard way of expressing calculus equations and problems.

However, lest you believe that Leibniz was completely innocent, you should know that he had no qualms about attacking Newton's character as well. Leibniz called Newton's theory of gravity an "occult quality," saying it seemed like magic that objects could pull on objects thousands of miles away with no other force at play. While accusing your rival of black magic may seem silly now, at the time (and considering all the genuinely magic-related work that Newton was doing) it was a valid accusation that could lead to a death sentence.

It didn't help that they came from two different and often rival countries (England and Germany), so the debate between them involved some national tensions! England was the last country in Europe to adopt Leibniz's notation for calculus, hundreds of years after the rest of Europe had decided that it was the preferable way of expressing it.

Did Isaac Newton Ever Marry?

As with all great historical figures, the question of Newton's sex life has come up more than once. As far as any written accounts (either by Newton, his friends, or his contemporary biographers) can tell us, he never married. In fact, not only did he never marry, but he seems to have never had any sustained relationships with any women at all.

In 1700, some records suggest that he was pursuing a courtship with a wealthy widow. Widows were seen as very desirable marriage prospects in the Medieval and Renaissance periods, since they could own their husband's property. Newton was certainly wealthy and eminent enough to have been an attractive prospect himself, even though he was almost sixty years old. It is unknown why the courtship never materialized into marriage.

Unsurprisingly for any unmarried man of significant historical fame, speculation has been raised that Newton might have been homosexual. However, evidence of meaningful relationships with men in his life is just as scanty as evidence of meaningful relationships with women.

Some of Newton's commonplace books write about his efforts to banish all sexual thoughts from his mind. It is not impossible that some of these thoughts might have been homosexual in nature, which would have been extremely taboo at the time – in other words, anyone in their right mind would have been trying to banish them, or else risk execution. However, more people seem to think it likely that Newton simply considered sexuality to be a distraction from his work. He would not be the only great mind in history that saw sex as a distraction from science. After all, pursuing sexual relationships can take up a lot of time and mental energy that Newton could have instead dedicated to his studies and experiments.

The general scholarly consensus, based on accounts of Newton's life, including those of his commonplace books, friends, and contemporary biographers, is that he never had any sort of extended contact with any woman outside of his family. If he had any romantic relationships with men, it might have flown under the radar on account of it being so much less expected. However, due to the lack of evidence and the anti-sex notes written in Newton's commonplace books, you will find Newton on many lists of "famous historical figures who died virgins."

The Gold Standard

Newton didn't just do work with math and science – he also ended up being a bit of an economist! In the later part of his life, Newton became involved in the Treasury of England, and in 1696, he became the warden of the Royal Mint, which was in charge of creating and controlling all the money that was made in England. While he was working there, he took charge of what was called the "great re-coinage," a process of replacing all the coins that had become worn-out, or that had been clipped and re-hammered as a means of counterfeiting.

Before this time, all of England's money had been made out of silver, and most coins were hand-made, which made them very easy to fake. They could be filed down around the edges and the filings re-pressed to make multiple coins that looked the same, but weighed different amounts. Low-ranking business people took these coins, judging their value based on their approximate size, but when they went to have them changed at a bank, they were informed that they had been cheated, and banks refused to pay them the difference. It is estimated that about 10% of all of England's currency was forged by the time Newton took on the project of fixing the situation.

Another problem was that the value of coins in England was no longer equivalent to the value of silver in the rest of Europe. This meant that English people could make more money by melting down their coins and selling them to continental Europeans than they could by actually using those coins to buy and sell things at home.

The whole situation was an economic disaster, and the Royal Mint looked to Newton to come up with a solution to the problem... which he did.

First, Newton disguised himself as a commoner and went wandering through the taverns of London and other major urban centres. At these taverns, he asked around about counterfeiting, gathering witnesses and counterfeiters under the pretense of wanting to buy counterfeit money. Once he had compiled his list of suspects, he took it upon himself to charge them, as a Justice of the Peace in England. For a year and a half, he interviewed and cross-examined more than a hundred people involved in the counterfeiting and witnesses who claimed they had information. By the end of this period of interrogations, he had convicted twenty-eight people who were making counterfeit money.

But during all of this, another shift was taking place in England. They were still paying for all their imports in silver, since silver was more valuable in continental Europe than it was in England. But they were also getting paid in gold for all their exports – gold which was only occasionally used as money in England itself. This led to a shortage of silver and an overabundance of gold in the English marketplace.

This led to one of Newton's other great projects: the establishment of a gold standard, rather than a silver standard, in England.

The terms "gold standard" and "silver standard" simply refer to ways to calculate the worth of money in a relatively impartial way. Essentially, a price was decided for a certain weight of metal, and then fractions of that weight of metal were worth equal fractions of that price. For example, if you decided that one kilogram of gold was worth a thousand dollars, then each gram of gold would be worth one dollar, so a ten-dollar coin could be made out of ten grams of gold.

England had been on a silver standard, while the rest of Europe was on a gold standard, which was causing difficulties in their imports and exports. Newton wrote a report to the Lord Commissioners of His Majesty's Treasury in 1717, explaining this problem. As a result, over the coming years, the silver standard was slowly phased out in England. However, it wasn't until over a hundred years later that it was dissolved completely, after a serious silver shortage in the 1790s and several years of economic turmoil as a result. England adopted the gold standard completely in 1844, a hundred and twenty-seven years after Newton's report brought the idea into people's minds.

Isaac Newton, Alchemy, and Magic

Some people have claimed that the reason that Newton became interested in working at the Royal Mint was not out of any interest in helping England economically, but because of one of his side projects: his attempts to discover the philosopher's stone.

While today, the philosopher's stone is mostly known for its appearance in J. K. Rowling's *Harry Potter* series, it is actually a very ancient idea in the field of study known as *alchemy*.

Alchemy was a precursor to modern chemistry. In fact, the word "chemist" actually first appeared as a shortened version of the word "alchemist." Alchemy is the study of the properties of different substances, and how those substances could interact with each other to form new substances or surprising reactions.

Experiments that we would describe as "alchemy" were first practiced in ancient Egypt, around 300 BC. It combined scientific and technological experiments with philosophical and religious explanations, attempting to develop theories about the world based on the experiments that were carried out to prove the properties of different substances. New appliances for conducting experiments (ones that bear strong resemblances to modern lab equipment) were developed in the first century AD by a woman called Maria Prophetissima, sometimes called "Mary the Prophetess" or "Mary the Jewess."

Sir Isaac Newton

Her experiments were written down almost three hundred years later by Zosimos of Panopolis, the first known writer of alchemical books.

In these early days, almost anything involving experiments and explanations was known as alchemy. However, in the Middle Ages, two main tasks became the focus of alchemy as a form of study. It was claimed that alchemists were only interested in two things: finding the secret to eternal life, and turning common metals like lead into pure gold.

Now is a good time to remember that the universe was understood in Europe, at this time, based mainly on the scientific ideas that Aristotle put forward in Ancient Greece – and in Aristotle's understanding of the world, the idea that one could turn lead into gold made perfect sense.

According to Aristotle, different substances had different properties – they were situated somewhere on a two-axis graph of hotness/coldness and wetness/dryness. For example, fire was very hot and very dry, while water was very cold and very wet. Other substances were in different places on that graph – for example, basil is hot and dry, but not as hot as cinnamon. Lead was cold and dry, while gold was hot and dry.

According to this principle, by changing the essential hot/cold and wet/dry alignment of a substance, you can change the substance itself. So, to turn lead into gold, you would have to heat it – not just heat it by holding it over a fire, but sort of "cosmically" heat it, in such a powerful way that its essential properties changed. It would be difficult, but it was theoretically possible.

In the modern day, we usually dismiss this kind of experiment as impossible, and it's easy to laugh at anyone who ever

Isaac Newton, Alchemy, and Magic

believed that they could do such magical acts. However, in the 1600s, alchemy was the most advanced scientific practice happening in Europe, so it really shouldn't be surprising that it caught Newton's interest.

Unlike the type of study that was happening in universities at the time, alchemy promoted what we would now call the "scientific method" – the technique of using experiments to figure out larger rules about how things work. This appealed to Newton, who was using this method for most of his studies at the time.

But there were more dangers for would-be alchemists than just the fact that their experiments might not work – in 1404, making gold or silver without governmental approval was made into a crime in England. Newton wrote extensively on the subject of alchemy, including its supposed ability to turn other metals into gold, but he was unable to publish any of his works during his lifetime for fear of being criminally prosecuted.

He did keep extensive notes on his study of alchemy. In the 1880s, a huge stack of his notes were dismissed as having "no scientific value" by some especially rational Victorians and put into storage, where they stayed for fifty years. In 1936, they were purchased by John Maynard Keynes, one of the most important economists and thinkers of the twentieth century. These notes included his notes and ideas about God, the Bible, alchemical experiments, and other types of magic. After studying the notes, Keynes wrote a speech called "Newton, the Man" which was presented by Keynes' brother at the three hundredth anniversary of Newton's birth. In this speech, Keynes famously said:

Sir Isaac Newton

> Newton was not the first of the age of reason. He was the last of the magicians, the last of the Babylonians and Sumerians, the last great mind which looked out on the visible and intellectual world with the same eyes as those who began to build our intellectual inheritance rather less than ten thousand years ago.

Since Keynes' speech was made public, much more interest has been sparked in Newton's studies into the occult. "Occult" is a blanket term for a variety of different magical topics. It comes from a Latin word that literally means "secret," and it is used to describe a wide range of magical, mystical, and non-traditionally religious practices. In the 1600s, anything that could get you in trouble with the church could be lumped under the label "occult," and Newton certainly studied a lot of things that could have gotten him in trouble with the church, if the church had ever dared to meddle with him.

Newton's Religious Beliefs

For example, he held some religious beliefs that were seen as extremely shocking. He did not accept the Christian doctrine of the Trinity (the concept of Father, Son, and Holy Ghost as all being the same God, or aspects of the same God) – instead, Newton adhered to a version of Christian doctrine about the role of Jesus Christ that had been considered heretical for hundreds of years. The belief was called *Arianism*, which says that Jesus is a lesser being than God the Father. This is still a controversial opinion in many Christian circles, but in the 1600s, saying such a belief out loud was grounds for execution.

He also laughed at the idea of the Devil, claiming that it was obviously just a way to try to make people fearful and more likely to listen to priests. This belief is even less controversial today than Arianism is – even many orthodox Christians today reject the idea of a sentient embodiment of all that is evil walking the earth. However, in Newton's day, thousands of witch-burnings were sweeping through Europe (and the Americas), and stories about the phenomenal power of the Devil were everywhere. Perhaps it was the overblown, melodramatic stories of baby-eating demons and satanic orgies that made Newton dismiss the idea that the Devil could be a real creature – he just seemed *too* powerful for a powerful and loving God to have created.

Sir Isaac Newton

Newton was also involved in the Freemasons, a society of men dating back to the times of the Crusades, which was created in order to try to preserve ancient wisdom. He became more involved in the Freemason Brotherhood as he grew older – coincidentally, as he became more and more reclusive, and less and less involved with the Christian church. The Masons supported Newton's experiments, in spite of their unorthodox results. Newton created the Royal Society of London for Improving Natural Knowledge along with some of the other Freemasons, and it was very strongly influenced by their values and their beliefs in ancient wisdom.

When he wasn't trying alchemical experiments or working with the Freemasons to preserve texts about magic from the ancient world, Newton was making predictions about key events in the Bible, and when they might happen (or might have happened). He identified the date of Jesus Christ's crucifixion as April 3, in the year 33 AD. He also predicted that the Apocalypse would occur in the year 2060 – which seemed like an infinitely far away date at the time, but is sneaking up pretty close on us! However, don't get too worried about Newton's dates – he also predicted the Second Coming of Jesus Christ in 1948.

Newton's work in the fields of magic, alchemy, Bible studies, and the occult are far less well-known than his scientific advancements. Part of this was because he had to keep them hidden during his life for his own safety, and part of it was because later scholars tended to want to avoid these parts of Newton's history. It certainly conflicts with the popular image of Newton as a great thinker and man of reason when you see him instead as, as Keynes put it, "the last of the magicians." However, in recent decades, there has been an upsurge of interest in Newton's magical research, with multiple books being written on the topic. By studying this, historians hope to gain more insight into the framework that Newton was using to understand the world – and by doing so, come to understand Newton himself and his experiments more clearly.

Newton's Final Years

In 1693, Newton suffered from what has since been referred to as his "Black Year." The "Black Year" was a mental breakdown that slowly devolved over the course of many months, until Newton was essentially incapacitated by fear, paranoia, depression, and insomnia. He alienated his friends by accusing them of conspiring to ruin his reputation or his life. This was long before the concept of mental illness was understood, and Newton's distress could only be defined as him "going mad" – a catch-all term that told people nothing except that they should be slightly fearful of the madman.

During this time, Newton cut off almost all his contact with the outside world. He had never had a large circle of friends or family, but during his "Black Year," he was almost completely isolated, and many of his old acquaintances feared that it was the end for the great scientist.

Fortunately, the "Black Year" was temporary, and Newton did recover his faculties. It took a year for him to regain his old personality, and the "Black Year" seemed to leave some marks that never quite healed, but after that year was over, he was able to let go of some of the fear and paranoia that had plagued him.

Once he recovered somewhat, Newton became aware of how strongly he had alienated the people who cared about him. He wrote extensive letters to his friends, apologizing for his behaviour and his accusations. Then he threw himself with renewed vigor into the study of magic, which he had laid aside for some time for the publication of his book, the *Principia*. It was during the period immediately following his "Black Year" that Newton wrote many of the papers about magic that were later purchased by Keynes.

While many people thought that the "Black Year" would mark the end of Newton's career – at least his career in the public eye – they couldn't have been more wrong. He went on to continue some of his most important public work after this year.

In 1703, Newton was elected president of the Royal Society of London for Improving Natural Knowledge. This gave him far more political power than he'd become accustomed to – the power to bring his knowledge and worldview to the rest of the world. It was during the time that he was president of the Royal Society that the scientific community slowly started to adopt the principles that Newton had based his work around: the creation and rigorous testing of theories. He promoted experiments, and the world slowly became more interested in them.

For about a decade, Newton enjoyed staggering success, both in his position as president of the Royal Society and in his work. However, he reached a hurdle in 1705 when he was accused of plagiarizing Gottfried Leibniz's research.

The accusation of plagiarism led to a seven-year legal battle. While Newton was eventually exonerated, the legal battle took a toll on his mental health once again, and he became increasingly excitable and paranoid about people trying to steal his fame. He was one of the most famous and successful thinkers in the entire western world, and yet he was plagued by distrust and suspicion.

In 1722, at the age of eighty (a shockingly old age for anyone to live to at the time), Newton began to suffer from a range of physical ailments. He became confined to his home, unwilling to eat (or unable to stomach) anything but vegetables and clear broth, which left him weak. He developed gout, bladder stones, and hemorrhoids. He spent his later years confined to his home, able to study, but do little else. Five years after the initial weakness, in March of 1727, Newton became unconscious and died some hours later.

His funeral was spectacularly extravagant. Even though he was only a high-ranking commoner in birth, his coffin was carried by noblemen and set in Westminster Abbey, a space reserved for the greatest figures of English history. A contemporary reporter on the scene described Newton's funeral as being "fit for a king."

Newton's Students

Newton's success and fame after his death was helped by some of his significant students. Roger Cotes proofread the *Principia* for Newton, and collaborated him on a set of rules about numerical analysis called the "Newton-Cotes formulae." Cotes developed his own formula as well (called "Euler's formula") for explaining a relationship between real and imaginary numbers. This formula is well-regarded enough that the famous twentieth century physicist Richard Feynman called it "the most remarkable formula in mathematics."

Newton's other extremely famous student was William Whiston, who was one of the people who was most responsible for popularizing Newton's ideas. He was interested in history and theology as well as math and science. While Newton was rather reluctant to talk publically about his religious beliefs, for fear of being persecuted, Whiston was an active proponent of the ideas that he and Newton shared about religion. They both believed in Arianism, arguing that Jesus Christ and God the Father were separate beings, and that Jesus was a lesser being than God the Father.

Whiston wrote a three-volume set of memoirs, which were one of the major works that historians used to reconstruct Newton's life. Professionally, they were obviously attached, with Whiston even taking over Newton's job as the Lucasian Professor of Mathematics at the University of Cambridge when

Newton became unable to hold it anymore. However, it is unclear how close they were personally. Newton may also have disliked Whiston's explicit religious views, and distanced himself from him to avoid getting caught up in a religious debate that he was not interested in being a part of. At one point, Whiston claimed that Newton was suspicious of him because he was too independent to be a good student. However, they maintained a relationship for a significant period of time.

William Stukeley was the third of Newton's significant contemporaries to contribute to his legacy. Stukeley was best known for his development of archeological techniques. Specifically, unlike previous historians, he preferred to visit historical sights and interview significant people rather than relying on sources that other people wrote. He developed a long-term friendship with Newton, and wrote a memoir describing their relationship and interactions in 1752, thirty years after Newton's death. This memoir, which is called *Memoirs of Sir Isaac Newton's Life*, is generally considered the authoritative source of information about Newton – especially about his personality and his personal life. Stukeley took great pains to humanize the scientist, and bring his genius to life, while always complimenting and praising his brilliance. Stukeley was also the first one to write about the story of an apple inspiring Newton's idea for the theory of gravity. It would not be an exaggeration to say that the apple myth is a major contributing factor to Newton's continuing fame – it's a recognizable story that sticks in people's minds far more than an invention or a mathematical formula.

Isaac Newton's Legacy

In his own day, Isaac Newton was famous. He was one of the earliest "scientist celebrities" in the modern world (a category that now includes the likes of Benjamin Franklin and Albert Einstein). But as famous and successful as he was in his own day, he could have had no idea of the stature he would reach after his death. Today, Newton is a touchstone of not just scientific knowledge, but pop-culture knowledge. The portrait of the aging man with long, flowing hair is instantly recognizable in a way that a picture of Robert Hooke could never be (and not *just* because Newton probably had all his pictures destroyed). Newton being hit on the head with an apple is one of the most famous images in scientific popular history. The laws that Newton articulated and the things that he invented are still in constant use and taught in high school science classes all over the world.

However, any figure who achieves this kind of historical prominence faces a problem: their personality becomes entirely overshadowed by their inventions. Today, "Newton the man" has been almost completely replaced in the popular consciousness with "Newton the scientist." To be fair, this is a transition that Newton himself tried to develop during his life, as he eschewed human relationships for scientific work.

Newton's most continuingly important inventions include his reflecting telescope (which was a far more efficient style of telescope than the ones that the most advanced scientists were using at the time), calculus (which he used to study change and curves, like the curves of the movements of the planets), the laws of motion, and the law of universal gravitation. Scientists and amateur stargazers alike still use the reflecting telescope to view the sky. High schools offer courses in calculus, and it is understood to be vital to anyone who is pursuing the study of math or science. And, of course, the three laws of motion and the law of universal gravitation are so famous that even many children can quote them, and it is impossible to pursue a study of science without knowing about them.

Because of his contributions, Newton became known as "the father of modern science." Every significant scientific advance that came after Newton seemed to rely, to some degree or another, on the incredible work that he did during his life. His scientific advances pushed science out of the rut that it had fallen into in the Middle Ages and Renaissance, into the new age that would be known as the "Enlightenment."

One of the reasons that Newton made such an impact on science was that he was among the first scientists to make serious progress through experiments rather than simply by reading the works of others and making educated guesses based on the principles that they explained. This process of reading and then reasoning based on what one read was the keystone of scientific thought in the Renaissance, and Newton's methods were considered unusual and even shocking – which is why he did not do as well in school as one might expect from such a genius.

Newton's interest in experimentation to find out information was related to his apprenticeship with William Clarke, the apothecary. Clarke helped Newton understand how science could help people, but also how failing to experiment and try new things could cause a problem (after all, if you keep giving people the same ineffective medicine, you're going to lose a lot of customers very quickly). Newton's experimentation techniques were also spurred on by his interest in the study of alchemy, which was the one field of science that had, at the time, *always* been focussed on experiments rather than conjecture.

During the Enlightenment, the period that essentially started with Newton's lifetime, conducting experiments became the favoured way to find out new information. The Scientific Method, which relies on making predictions that can be tested and then testing them, could only have been developed after Newton showed the world how important experiments really are to gathering new information. The Scientific Method became the preferred method of study in the Enlightenment period, and continues to be the method that scientists use to gather accurate information today.

Newton's Enlightenment ideas also ended up having an impact on politics. Kelly Cline argues that Newton's ideas actually helped spur on the American and French revolutions, more than fifty years after Newton's death. She argues that Newton achieved what mathematicians had been seeking since the dawn of time: he unlocked the mathematical formulae that controlled the universe. His laws of gravitation and motion explained things that had previously been seen as great intractable mysteries of the universe.

Once these mysteries had been unravelled, people started to see the world with a lot more suspicion and skepticism. It made people look more critically at each other's behaviour, even the behaviour of high-powered individuals. "If there are natural laws for how planets move," Cline asks, "shouldn't there be natural laws for how people should act as well?"

Sir Isaac Newton

People became far less tolerant of tyranny and perceived injustice, and far more willing to rebel against leaders and monarchs who were treating their subjects unfairly. It was because of this, Cline reasons, that people in the eighteenth and nineteenth centuries became so interested in overthrowing corrupt rulers. This remains part of Newton's legacy to this day.

After Newton died, he attained even higher levels of praise than he had enjoyed during his life, as his good ideas came to the forefront of people's memories. Some of the less pleasant parts of his personality (which were present even in Stukeley's highly admiring description of his life) faded away almost entirely. Newton has been elevated almost to the status of a god by subsequent thinkers, both scientists and artists. The famous English poet and artist, William Blake, painted a famous portrait of Newton as a Greek god in 1795 that, while more dramatic than most representations of the scientist, certainly did not represent an unusual way of seeing him.

Today, most people see Newton as the god-like figure Blake painted. But it's important to remember that he was a real person too, who lived and died and had his own beliefs and concerns besides his interest in science. By learning more about Newton the man, we can develop a greater understanding of the context in which he developed his famous inventions and scientific theories. And by learning about how he developed his theories, maybe we can also learn how we too can be the kind of great minds that can contribute to the scientific discourse that Newton created.

Printed in Poland
by Amazon Fulfillment
Poland Sp. z o.o., Wrocław